Schizoid Per: Disorder

Complete Guide to Understanding and Living with Schizoid Personality Disorder

Sara Cross

Table of Contents

Introduction

The rain beat a staccato rhythm against Elias' window, each drop a punctuation mark in the symphony of his solitude. Inside, bathed in the soft glow of a reading lamp, he sat like a monk in his self-made monastery, books his only companions. Elias wasn't lonely, not in the way most understood. He reveled in the silence, the absence of expectations, the freedom to exist in his own orbit, untouched by the cacophony of human interaction.

He had grown up a curious anomaly, a child who found playground chatter grating and eye contact an unwelcome intrusion. While other children built sandcastles, he constructed intricate labyrinths in his mind, peopled by characters from forgotten epics. His parents, bewildered but loving, watched him retreat further into his inner world, a solitary satellite in their family constellation.

School was a necessary nuisance, a daily gauntlet of forced interactions and stifling routines. Elias learned to navigate it with stoic detachment, a ghost at the edges of classrooms, unnoticed or misconstrued. It was easier to wear a mask of indifference, to let others fill in the blanks with their own assumptions, than to explain the intricate tapestries woven within his mind.

He found solace in books, portals to worlds where solitude wasn't a burden but a badge of honor. He roamed the desolate plains of ancient Rome with Stoic philosophers, scaled the icy peaks of the Himalayas with Tibetan monks, and danced with ghosts in gothic novels. Through their words, he found a kinship with kindred spirits, their words echoing the quiet song of his own soul.

Years passed, seasons blurring like pages in a forgotten book. Elias became a librarian, a custodian of stories, a silent curator of forgotten narratives. The hushed sanctuary of the library was his haven, the smell of old paper and leather a comforting balm. He spoke little, his words carefully measured, each one a precious gem unearthed from the mines of his introspective mind.

One day, a woman named Clara stumbled into his world, drawn by the quiet hum of his existence. Unlike others who recoiled from his aloofness, Clara saw through the façade, glimpsed the vibrant landscape hidden behind his guarded eyes. She spoke in whispers, respected his silences, and found beauty in the unspoken nuances of his expression.

Their connection was a slow waltz, an unspoken symphony of shared glances and gentle smiles. In her presence, Elias found a flicker of warmth, a hesitant desire to step out of his self-imposed exile. With her, conversations weren't a chore, but a shared exploration, tentative steps into a world he'd long believed he was better off without.

Clara became his bridge, a gentle hand guiding him back to the shores of human connection. He learned to laugh again, the sound rusty at first, then blossoming into a melody that filled the empty corners of his soul. He discovered the joy of shared silences, the comfort of knowing someone understood the language of his unspoken thoughts.

Their journey wasn't without its hurdles. Social gatherings remained daunting, his natural inclination always pulling him back to the solace of solitude. But with Clara's unwavering support, he learned to take small steps, each one a victory dance in the quiet battlefield of his own mind.

Elias' story wasn't a cure, not a fairytale ending where the hermit throws off his cloak and joins the boisterous carnival of life. It was a slow, deliberate unfurling, a gradual acceptance of the beauty that existed both within the walls of his solitude and in the hesitant steps towards connection. It was a testament to the power of understanding, of accepting that different ways of being are not flaws, but facets of the rich tapestry of human experience.

His book, born from the embers of his unique journey, was a gentle guide, a map for those who navigated the uncharted waters of Schizoid Personality Disorder. It wasn't a manual for conformity, but a celebration of individuality, a whisper of hope that connection, in its myriad forms, was possible even for those who found solace in the quiet hum of their own solitude.

For Elias, the rain continued to fall, but now it was a lullaby, a gentle reminder that even in the quietest corners, life bloomed in its own exquisite way. And in the soft glow of his reading lamp, as he poured his experiences onto the page, he knew that somewhere, another soul might find solace in his words, another wanderer might glimpse a familiar star in the vast constellation of his being.

Chapter 1: Deciphering Schizoid Personality Disorder: A Comprehensive Overview of Its Nature and Importance

In conversations about mental health, schizoid personality disorder (SPD) is frequently hidden behind mists and misunderstandings. It's not about schizophrenia or split personalities; rather, it's about a particular pattern of conduct marked by a strong distancing from social interactions and a strong need for isolation. We need to examine SPD's fundamental characteristics, investigate its possible causes, and acknowledge its importance in the larger context of human experience if we are to comprehend it fully.

Exploring SPD's Inner World:

Emotional Detachment: The repressed experience and expression of emotions is the hallmark of SPD. People who have SPD frequently find it difficult to emotionally connect with others, coming across as aloof or uncaring. They may find the depth of human emotions to be too much for them, and their inner world appears remote.

Social Withdrawal and Limited Relationships: Due to their emotional distancing, people with SPD frequently value their alone time and steer clear of intimate connections. They can find engaging in social situations taxing and instead favor solitary pastimes or introspective pursuits. Not only are sexual connections uncommon, but forming and sustaining friendships can be extremely difficult.

Rich Inner World and Vivid Imagination: People with SPD frequently have a thriving inner life in spite of their social withdrawal. They might indulge in elaborate daydreams, explore philosophical ideas, or find comfort in artistic endeavors. Their brains turn into a haven where they can escape the difficulties of social engagement.

Investigating the SPD Seedlings:

Developmental Influences: Early life events can have a significant impact on how SPD develops. Emotional detachment and social disengagement can arise as a result of connection disruptions, emotional neglect, or an overemphasis on independence. Trauma, either witnessed or experienced, can reinforce these tendencies even more.

Biological and Genetic Factors: Although studies on the biological foundations of SPD are still in progress, certain data points to the possibility that neurotransmitters and heredity may have an impact on personality characteristics. Relevant factors could also include unique temperamental predispositions or a family history of mental health issues.

Environmental and Psychosocial Factors: SPD expression can be influenced by the constant interaction between a person's innate tendencies and their surroundings. Social disengagement and the ability to use healthy coping strategies can be made worse by social isolation, a lack of community support, and unfavorable cultural attitudes toward mental health.

Why SPD Is Important:

Empathy and comprehension: Fostering empathy and creating a supporting network with those who have SPD requires an awareness of and comprehension of SPD. It's important to recognize their particular struggles and provide environments where they feel understood and embraced rather than pathologizing or labeling them.

Tackling Misconceptions: Unfounded beliefs about SPD, such as comparing it to schizophrenia or depicting sufferers as innately dangerous, reinforce stigma and impede the availability of appropriate care. Dispelling these rumors is crucial to encouraging acceptance and encouraging the behavior of seeking assistance.

Individual Strengths and Growth: Despite the difficulties SPD might bring, it's critical to recognize the potential benefits this style of being can offer. People with SPD can be incredibly creative, independent thinkers, and profound thinkers. They can live happy, full lives on their terms if these strengths are acknowledged and developed.

Supporting Relationship Choices: Although intimate partnerships might be difficult for people with SPD, it's important to recognize that they still require a connection of some kind. Encouraging meaningful relationships, whether with friends, family, or virtual communities, while also honoring their preference for solitude can contribute to their general well-being.

To sum up, Schizoid Personality Disorder is a spectrum of experiences rather than a binary diagnosis. We can get above stigma and prejudices by examining its essential characteristics, investigating its possible causes, and appreciating its importance. This knowledge opens the door to empathy, knowledgeable assistance, and the recognition of each person's unique abilities within the particular context of human experiences.

Chapter 2: Schizoid Personality Disorder (SPD): An Exploration of Its Fundamental Elements

Gaining insight into the inner workings of Schizoid Personality Disorder (SPD) necessitates close observation and sophisticated comprehension. Here, we go more deeply into the three characteristics that best capture this distinct style of being:

1. Limited Expressiveness and Emotional Detachment:

A Muted Landscape: People with SPD experience emotions that are simmering beneath the surface. They frequently talk of experiencing a dulled intensity of joy, grief, rage, and even love, along with a sensation of emotional numbness. Their facial expressions often reflect this distance, frequently coming across as lifeless or uninteresting.

The Paradox of Inner Richness: Although an individual's emotions may appear subdued on the outside, their inner world may be a complex web of ideas and sensations. They might delve into the depths of their imagination for comfort, ponder philosophical ideas, or have vivid daydreams in which they experience rich emotional landscapes on the inside.

Difficulties in Connection: Emotionally connecting with others is a difficult task. It might be intimidating to share vulnerabilities, show empathy, or negotiate the subtleties of social interactions. This can impede the growth of intimate connections by giving the impression that you are distant or icy.

2. Social Disengagement and Restricted Connections:

Solitude as Sanctuary: People with SPD find security and comfort in being by themselves. Social interactions can be overwhelming and taxing, requiring a lot of energy and leaving one feeling exhausted. It can be draining to participate in big events or stay in touch with people daily, which makes them value their hobbies and alone time.

Minimalistic Social Circles: Close friendships and sexual relationships are frequently absent or ephemeral, but some people with SPD may retain weak social ties with family or coworkers. Sustaining the emotional vulnerability and commitment necessary for these kinds of relationships can be taxing and ultimately disappointing.

Navigating Expectations: People with SPD may experience challenges as a result of society's emphasis on social interaction. They may experience emotions of alienation and loneliness as a result of social pressure to fit in and misconceptions about their need for privacy.

3. Mental Models and Internal Environment:

Bright Imagination and Rich Inner Life: There is a rich inner world that exists beyond the difficulties of social connection. People with SPD frequently have vivid imaginations and indulge in elaborate daydreams and magical worlds. They may find comfort and a sense of escape from the oppressive demands of social life in this rich internal world.

Philosophical Inquiry and Abstract Thinking: They might have an innate propensity for philosophical inquiry and abstract thinking, considering ideas such as existence, meaning, and the nature of reality. For them, profound intellectual pursuits or philosophical conversations can be immensely fulfilling.

Detachment and Observation: People with SPD frequently take on the role of the detached observer, pondering and evaluating their surroundings without always feeling compelled to take an active part. They can negotiate the intricacies of interpersonal contact and retain a certain emotional distance from social events because of their observant position.

Understanding these fundamental characteristics helps us better comprehend the distinctive experiences of people with SPD. It's critical to keep in mind that this is a range of options rather than a strict checklist. Since each person will display these traits differently, it is important to acknowledge each person's unique strengths and complexities to develop empathy, provide support, and create lasting relationships.

Chapter 3: Schizoid Personality Disorder (SPD) and Developmental Factors

Early childhood events are typically considered to be a fruitful ground for the seeds of Schizoid Personality Disorder (SPD). Even though the precise causes are still unknown and complex, knowing the possible developmental impacts might help clarify how its essential characteristics came to be.

1. Emotional Abuse and Disruptions of Attachment:

The Significance of Secure Attachment: A caregiver's warmth, responsiveness, and constant emotional availability are signs of a secure attachment, which is essential to a child's proper emotional growth. Early attachment disruptions (emotional maltreatment, inconsistent parenting, parental absence) can impede the development of emotional intimacy and trust in people with SPD.

Emotional Detachment as a Coping Mechanism: Children who do not receive consistent emotional support may learn to emotionally distance themselves as a coping strategy. Although this distance can protect individuals from more suffering and disappointment, it also limits their capacity to connect with people completely and feel the whole gamut of emotions.

Internalizing the "Not-Me" Self: Children who experience persistent unmet emotional needs may learn to believe that their feelings are unwanted or unimportant. As a result, individuals may feel cut off from their own emotions and come to believe that they are "not meant" for intimate relationships.

2. Overemphasis on Self-Sufficiency and Independence:

Early Encouragement of Autonomy: Some people with SPD describe upbringings in which self-reliance and independence were greatly prized. Although encouraging autonomy is essential for growth, placing too much focus on it might inhibit emotional expression and reliance on others, which may lead to social disengagement.

Internalizing the "Lone Wolf" Ideal: A youngster may internalize the "lone wolf" ideal if they are inundated with messages that emphasize independence and minimize the value of interpersonal relationships. Even as an adult, this may make it difficult to establish and maintain personal connections.

Loss of Opportunity for Emotional Learning: Placing too much emphasis on independence might deprive kids of important chances to develop their social skills, empathy, and emotional expression. These are the kinds of talents that come from emotional support and caring interactions, and they are essential for creating enduring bonds later in life.

3. Traumatic Events and Emotional Intolerance:

The Scars of Early Trauma: Childhood experiences of sexual, emotional, or physical abuse can have a significant effect on an individual's emotional growth. Trauma can cause feelings of dread, mistrust, and alienation, which might hinder one's capacity to build safe and dependable connections.

Persistent Family Disagreement and Instability: Being raised in a setting where there is a lot of conflict, stress, or emotional instability can make one feel insecure and unpredictable. This may exacerbate emotional disengagement and make it more difficult to meaningfully connect with people.

Emotional Regulation Difficulties: The development of good emotional regulation abilities can be hampered by trauma and ongoing stress. People with SPD may find it difficult to control their emotions, which makes them more likely to retreat and stay away from circumstances that make them feel uncomfortable.

It's crucial to keep in mind that these are only a few possible developmental factors for SPD. Each person's unique experiences and vulnerabilities play a part in the disorder's distinctive presentation. By being aware of these factors, we can develop empathy, provide knowledgeable assistance, and establish settings that promote tolerance and acceptance for those with SPD.

Chapter 4: Schizoid Personality Disorder (SPD): Environmental and Psychosocial Factors

While developmental experiences can be linked to the emergence of Schizoid Personality Disorder (SPD), this is not the whole picture. The expression and effects of SPD are significantly shaped by environmental and psychosocial factors during an individual's life.

1. Life Events and Challenges that are Stressful:

Social Isolation and Lack of Community Support: People with SPD may already find it difficult to form relationships and engage in social situations. These difficulties can be made worse by living in isolated areas or without access to caring groups, which can prolong the withdrawal cycle and make it more difficult for them to make new connections.

Cultural Expectations and Stigma Around Mental Health: People with SPD may be discouraged from getting treatment or forming deep connections as a result of negative cultural attitudes and misconceptions about mental health. They may become even more alone and unable to obtain resources and assistance due to their fear of being stigmatized and judged.

Discrimination and Rejection: People with SPD may be especially sensitive to discrimination or rejection because of perceived differences or social awkwardness. It may be more difficult for them to reach out for connection as a result of these events if they continue to feel alone and if they have unfavorable opinions of themselves.

2. Abuse and Trauma:

The Enduring Impact of Trauma: As was covered in the previous chapter, childhood trauma exposure can have a long-lasting negative influence on social development and emotional growth. Trauma can have an equally profound effect even if it happens later in life. It can show itself as increased distance, mistrust, and trouble establishing connections.

Retraumatization and Triggering locations: A person may experience emotional distress when they are in certain social circumstances or locations that serve as triggers, bringing up memories of past trauma. This may cause people with SPD to completely avoid situations of this nature, which would further reduce their social interactions and chances to form connections.

The Need for Trauma-Informed Support: It's critical to acknowledge the possible influence of trauma on the experiences of people with SPD. They can escape the avoidance pattern and create better connections with the assistance of trauma-informed support and safe spaces for recovery.

3. The Interaction of Environment and Personal Predispositions:

Vulnerability and Resilience: It's critical to keep in mind that there are differences in the vulnerability and resilience of people with SPD.

Some people might be more vulnerable to the harmful effects of their surroundings, whereas others might have learned useful coping skills or found support in unlikely places.

The Significance of Encouragement Settings: Establishing encouraging settings that honor personal preferences and requirements can have a big impact on people with SPD. This may entail providing flexible work schedules, encouraging remote work, or cultivating welcoming and empathetic social environments.

Building Personal Strengths and Resources: It's critical to identify and support the resources and strengths that each person with SPD possesses. Their capacity for independence, reflection, and creativity can be quite helpful in overcoming the difficulties presented by SPD and creating a meaningful existence.

Through comprehension of the interaction between environmental and psychosocial elements, we can transcend the narrow emphasis on individual vulnerabilities. Understanding the larger context of SPD enables us to push for systemic reforms that provide inclusive and encouraging environments for people with SPD, enabling them to realize their full potential and make meaningful connections with the outside world.

Chapter 5: Getting Through the Maze: Schizoid Personality Disorder Diagnosis and Evaluation (SPD)

To fully comprehend Schizoid Personality Disorder (SPD), one must delve into the fields of evaluation and diagnosis. This important chapter gives us the tools we need to investigate the diagnostic criteria, distinguish SPD from other illnesses, and learn about possible courses of treatment.

1. Using the DSM-5 Standards:

SPD can be diagnosed using a standardized framework that is provided by the Diagnostic and Statistical Manual of Mental Disorders, Fifth Edition (DSM-5). An individual must meet four out of the following criteria for at least a year to be diagnosed:

Reduced need for close connections and social interactions: This shows up as a predilection for isolation and a lack of enthusiasm for group activities.

Almost no pleasure in most activities: People with SPD frequently describe a muted sense of delight and struggle to find enjoyment in hobbies or social situations.

Limited, if any, emotional expression: They exhibit a limited or flat emotional expression range, coming across as aloof or uncaring even in highly charged situations.

Selection of solitary activities: Preference for solo pursuits like writing, reading, or relaxing in nature.

Few, if any, close friends or confidantes: They might not have many close friends or personal ties, nor many social connections.

Take little or no joy in sexual experiences: One of the most common characteristics of SPD is difficulty feeling or wanting sexual intimacy.

Irrespective of praise or criticism: People with SPD frequently lack motivation from outside approval or anxiety about being judged, which contributes to their social disengagement.

A sensation of numbness or emotional detachment: They talk about being cut off from both their own and other people's feelings.

A lack of enthusiasm in starting a family: People with SPD find it difficult to establish and sustain a family.

It's crucial to remember that these standards are not absolute and should be weighed against the person's general functioning and situations in life. To assess personality disorders, a thorough clinical evaluation that rules out concomitant diseases and takes into account other possible diagnoses is always necessary.

2. Distinctive Features from Other Disorders:

There are instances when the unique characteristics of SPD coincide with those of other mental health disorders. Making the distinction between them is essential for precise diagnosis and efficient care.

Social Anxiety Disorder: Social anxiety and SPD both refer to a feeling of unease in social settings. On the other hand, people with SPD usually have no desire for social connection at all, and people with social anxiety frequently experience extreme fear and anxiety in social situations.

Major Depressive Disorder: Social disengagement and a reduction in emotional expression are further symptoms of depression. It can be distinguished from SPD, though, by the existence of additional depressed symptoms such as low mood, exhaustion, and changes in eating and sleep patterns.

Autism Spectrum Disorder (ASD): People with ASD may also find it difficult to interact with others and may like solitary pursuits. Repetitive behaviors, as well as variations in communication and sensory processing, set ASD apart from SPD.

For SPD to be correctly diagnosed and distinguished from other potential disorders, a comprehensive evaluation comprising observations, questionnaires, and interviews should be performed by a qualified mental health practitioner.

3. Beyond the Label: Introspection and Individual Perception

Although receiving a formal diagnosis from a mental health professional is beneficial, people who want to learn more about themselves can also use self-assessment methods and websites. Online checklists and questionnaires can provide information on personal characteristics and actions that are consistent with SPD. It's crucial to keep in mind that self-assessment tools can be a useful starting point for introspection and seeking out additional guidance, but they should never be used in place of a professional diagnosis.

Labeling and diagnosing SPD is only one aspect of understanding it. Acknowledging one's obstacles and struggles in social interaction, emotional expression, and forming relationships can enable people to look for the right kind of assistance and investigate methods for leading satisfying lives despite the particular difficulties presented by SPD.

Chapter 6: Setting a Course: Schizoid Personality Disorder Treatment Options and Strategies

Even though Schizoid Personality Disorder (SPD) has its share of difficulties, there are resources and support networks available to help navigate the terrain. This chapter examines the wide range of approaches and techniques for treating SPD that are available to people, giving them the tools they need to set their path to improved health and personal fulfillment.

1. Psychotherapy Methodologies:

Individual Therapy: Establishing a rapport of trust with a therapist is essential to SPD treatment. A secure setting for examining triggers, fears, and issues with emotional expression is provided by individual therapy. Develop coping skills for social situations and challenge negative thought patterns with cognitive-behavioral therapy (CBT). Psychodynamic therapy helps people develop a stronger sense of self by exploring early experiences that might be causing current social withdrawal.

Group Therapy: While social engagement presents difficulties for people with SPD, taking part in a supportive group setting can have special advantages. Making connections with people who have gone through similar things to you can help you feel less alone, and more understanding, and give you chances to practice social skills in a controlled and safe setting.

2. Considerations for Medication:

Limited Role of Medication: The main characteristics of SPD, such as emotional detachment or social withdrawal, are not specifically addressed by medication. Nonetheless, some drugs may be useful in treating co-occurring disorders like anxiety or depression that could aggravate SPD symptoms.

Generally speaking, antipsychotic drugs are not advised for SPD unless co-occurring psychotic symptoms are evident.

3. Interventions to Provide Support:

Skills Training: For people with SPD who have trouble interacting with others, developing critical skills like communication, assertiveness, and emotional expression can be extremely important. In addition to specialized programs like social skills training that offer helpful frameworks and tactics for navigating social situations, these skills can be applied in individual or group therapy settings.

Creative Expression: For people with SPD, using creative mediums like writing, music, or art can be a very effective way to explore their emotions and learn about themselves. Taking part in creative pursuits can be a safe approach to exploring inner spaces, making emotional connections, and discovering new avenues for fulfillment and communication.

Building Community: Supporting connections with like-minded people or participation in online communities can help people with SPD feel understood and like they belong. Locating SPD support groups or online discussion boards might offer chances for peer assistance, experience sharing, and learning from one another's paths.

4. A Person-Centered Approach:

It's crucial to remember that each individual with SPD experiences the disorder differently and has unique needs and preferences. Treatment should be tailored to the individual's specific goals, strengths, and challenges. A collaborative approach involving the individual, therapist, and any other relevant support systems is essential for developing a comprehensive and effective treatment plan.

5. Embracing Individual Potential:

Living with SPD can be challenging, but it's important to recognize the potential for growth and fulfillment that exists within each individual. Focusing on personal strengths, interests, and creative pursuits can be empowering and lead to a meaningful and enriching life. By embracing their unique perspectives and ways of being, individuals with SPD can navigate their paths to personal well-being and find their forms of connection and belonging in the world.

Chapter 7: Navigating the Archipelago of Relationships: Building Meaningful Connections with Schizoid Personality Disorder

For individuals with Schizoid Personality Disorder (SPD), the concept of relationships can feel like a vast ocean dotted with scattered islands. While the yearning for connection may exist, navigating the complexities of social interaction and emotional intimacy can be daunting. This chapter explores the unique challenges and opportunities of relationship building for those with SPD, offering a compass to navigate these uncharted waters.

1. Intimate Relationships:

The Paradox of Intimacy: The desire for a close, emotionally fulfilling relationship can coexist with a fear of vulnerability and the overwhelming intensity of emotional entanglement. People who have SPD may be dreading the demands of intimacy but also yearning for company.

Communication Challenges: Navigating the complex intricacies of emotional communication and expressing feelings can be quite challenging. Misunderstandings brought on by a lack of expressiveness or a hard time interpreting social cues can impede the growth of trust and exacerbate feelings of loneliness.

Setting Boundaries and Managing Expectations: It's critical to set boundaries that honor each person's need for privacy as well as their partner's need for connection. Understanding and open communication are crucial for negotiating the special dynamics of a relationship with an individual who has SPD.

2. Social Circles and Friendships:

Finding the Right Fit: People with SPD may find comfort in relating to others who value their independence and are introverted as much as they are. Developing friendships with people who value their privacy and independence might help to create deep bonds without becoming burdensome.

Small Circles, Deep Bonds: While big parties can be exhausting, developing smaller networks of close friends or participating in activities with others who share your interests can offer chances for support and connection.

Social Skills Development: People with SPD can feel more at ease in social situations and fortify existing relationships by recognizing and using social skills including active listening, striking up discussions, and expressing gratitude.

3.   Juggling   Self-Sufficiency   with Interconnectedness:

Embracing the Need for Solitude: Prioritizing periods of solitude and engaging in activities that provide personal fulfillment is essential for individuals with SPD. Recognizing their unique need for alone time without guilt or judgment is crucial for maintaining emotional well-being.

Reaching Out When Needed: While independence is vital, acknowledging the need for occasional social interaction and reaching out for support when needed are important aspects of self-care. Connecting with trusted friends, family, or therapists can provide a sense of connection and prevent complete isolation.

Finding Creative Forms of Connection: Exploring alternative forms of connection, such as online communities, shared hobbies, or creative collaborations, can offer fulfilling ways to interact with others without compromising on personal needs and preferences.

4. Recognizing Individual Journeys:

It's important to remember that the path to meaningful connections for individuals with SPD is diverse and personal. Some may choose to prioritize solitude and focus on building inner fulfillment, while others may actively seek and cultivate close relationships. Respecting individual choices and celebrating the various ways of existing and connecting is key to fostering empathy and inclusion.

5. Building Bridges of Understanding:

For those supporting individuals with SPD, practicing patience, open communication, and active listening are key. Recognizing their unique needs and respecting their boundaries without compromising on their own are essential aspects of maintaining healthy relationships. Encouraging their interests, acknowledging their emotional expressions (however subtle), and providing support without pressure can be invaluable in fostering trusting and fulfilling connections.

Navigating the landscape of relationships with SPD can be a journey of exploration and acceptance. By recognizing the obstacles and embracing the potential, persons with SPD can construct bridges of connection and find their path to meaningful relationships, building islands of shared experience in the wide archipelago of human interaction.

Chapter 8: Accepting Uniqueness and Development: A Developing Path with Schizoid Personality Disorder

The final chapter of the book on Schizoid Personality Disorder (SPD) is not a conclusion, but rather an invitation to continue growing and embracing oneself on a journey that is still unfolding. SPD has difficulties, but it also has the potential to bring about personal fulfillment and a distinct perspective on the world.

1. Embracing and Appreciating Your Self:

Celebrating Strengths: People with SPD have innate strengths that are sometimes disregarded or misinterpreted. When accepted and encouraged, their independent attitude, introverted personality, and creative potential can be tremendous assets. Acknowledging and embracing these abilities as essential components of their own identities is vital for fostering self-worth and achieving personal satisfaction.

Challenging Negative Self-Perceptions: Societal expectations and misconceptions can contribute to internalized stigma and negative self-perceptions for individuals with SPD. Challenging these detrimental narratives and admitting the reality of their experiences are vital steps towards self-acceptance and appreciating their unique way of being.

Finding Meaning in Solitude: For individuals with SPD, solitude is not a cause of loneliness, but a sanctuary for self-exploration, renewal, and creative expression. Embracing their natural predisposition for isolation as a source of strength and personal pleasure allows individuals to thrive in ways that may differ from traditional societal expectations.

2. Continuous Learning and Personal Development:

Lifelong Learning: The pursuit of information, whether through official schooling, independent study, or personal discovery, can be a deeply gratifying experience for those with SPD. Their introspective temperament and intellectual curiosity can fuel their journey of continual learning and self-discovery.

Exploring Creative Outlets: Creative expression, whether via painting, music, writing, or other forms, offers a powerful outlet for emotional exploration and self-communication. Engaging in creative hobbies can allow individuals with SPD a safe space to express their inner worlds and connect with their emotions in a non-verbal way.

Embracing Personal Growth: Regardless of SPD, personal growth is a lifelong journey. Setting personal goals, challenging oneself in tiny ways, and appreciating even minor achievements can create a sense of purpose and joy. Encouraging and supporting individuals with SPD in their endeavors, however unique they may seem, encourages them to embrace their path of growth.

3. Navigating a Supportive Environment:

Empathy and Understanding: Creating surroundings that are tolerant, welcoming, and free from judgment is vital for assisting individuals with SPD. Recognizing their particular needs and preferences, respecting their limits, and cultivating open communication are crucial aspects of creating trust and facilitating their incorporation into social contexts.

Challenging Stigma and Misconceptions: Dismantling negative stereotypes and pushing for the understanding of SPD is crucial for creating a more inclusive and supportive world. Bias against SPD can be fought and acceptance can be promoted by educating the public and medical professionals about its complexity.

Celebrating Diversity of Experiences: There are countless distinct ways to be alive within the range of human experiences. Accepting and appreciating the variety of personalities, including those with SPD traits, broadens our understanding as a society and makes the world a more welcoming place for all.

The SPD journey is a rich tapestry woven with growth chances and challenges rather than a straight line. People with SPD can reach their full potential and discover their special place in the world by embracing their individuality, building on their strengths, and creating supportive circumstances. Recall that this is a call to action for all of us to embrace and appreciate the vast diversity of human experiences, not just their tale.

Our investigation into Schizoid Personality Disorder is now complete. Hopefully, this journey has given you a better grasp of its complexity, given you the confidence to dispel myths, and stoked your desire to make the world a more accepting and encouraging place for people with SPD and all those who manage diverse ways of being. As we come to the end of this chapter, let us not forget that each of us is on a journey to embrace our uniqueness and promote personal development. By traveling this path together, we can weave a more intricate and significant fabric of human experience.

Chapter 9: Supplemental Materials and Networks for People with Schizoid Personality Disorder

It can be difficult to live with or support someone who has Schizoid Personality Disorder (SPD), but there are a lot of tools and support groups available to provide connections and help. A list of helpful resources and communities for navigating the SPD experience is included in this chapter.

Links and Books:

The website of the National Education Alliance on Borderline Personality Disorder (NEABPD) provides in-depth details regarding SPD, including resources for families and people as well as symptoms, diagnosis, and treatment choices.

The International Society for the Study of Personality Disorders (ISSPD) is a valuable resource that offers educational materials and scientific research on personality disorders, including SPD.

Beatrice Chestnut's book "Understanding Schizoid Personality Disorder: A Guide for the Curious and Concerned": This book provides a kind and perceptive examination of SPD from both a professional and a personal standpoint.

Susan Cain's book "Quiet: The Power of Introverts in a World That Can't Stop Talking": Although it doesn't directly address SPD, it does discuss the advantages and disadvantages of introverted personalities, which may be relatable to those who have SPD.

Online Forums and Support Groups: Several online forums and support groups link people with SPD and their loved ones, facilitating peer support, experience sharing, and a secure environment for talking about struggles and victories.

Expert Assistance and Lobbying Organizations:

Mental health providers: Individual therapy, group therapy, and medication management can be provided for people with SPD by psychologists, psychiatrists, and therapists who specialize in personality disorders.

National Alliance on Mental Illness (NAMI): This group advocates for people and families dealing with mental illness, including SPD, and provides support groups, educational materials, and advocacy services.

The Jed Foundation: This group supports and helps people dealing with mental health issues, including SPD, and focuses on mental health in teens and young adults.

The Trevor Project: This group helps LGBTQ+ youth, especially those dealing with mental health issues like SPD, by offering crisis intervention and suicide prevention services.

Keep in mind:

There may be more resources in your neighborhood; this is not an exhaustive list.

Getting expert assistance is essential for overcoming SPD's obstacles and creating useful coping strategies.

For people with SPD and their loved ones, support groups and online forums can provide invaluable peer support and a sense of community.

Advocacy groups are essential in eradicating the stigma associated with SPD and fostering a more compassionate and accepting environment for those who suffer from this personality disorder.

Through the utilization of available resources, professional help, and developing relationships with supportive groups, people with SPD can effectively negotiate the challenges associated with the disease and establish a purposeful and happy existence. Never forget that there is help available at every turn and that you are not alone.

Appendix: Key Terms for Schizoid Personality Disorder Glossary

Attachment: The emotional connection that develops between a baby and its caregiver and serves as the basis for the baby's later social and emotional growth.

Comorbid: The existence of two or more mental health disorders that co-occur in the same person.

Coping mechanisms: Techniques for handling uncomfortable feelings, tension, or demanding circumstances.

Diagnosis: The process of determining, using standards from diagnostic guides such as the DSM-5, a particular mental health disorder.

Emotional detachment: A muted sensation and expression of feelings that frequently come out as chilly or uncaring.

Emotional expression: How people speak and express their feelings to other people.

Introversion: A personality attribute that is sometimes contrasted with extroversion, it is defined by a penchant for introspection and solitude.

Misconceptions: Untrue or incorrect ideas regarding a specific subject or phenomenon.

Personality disorder: a collection of persistent personality traits that cause distress or functional impairment and markedly depart from social standards.

Social anxiety disorder: Severe fear and anxiety in social settings is the hallmark of this mental illness.

Social withdrawal is the preference for isolation over social connection.

Stigma: Discrimination and prejudice connected to a specific ailment or population.

Support groups: Congregations of people who understand and support one another based on a shared experience, such as dealing with a particular mental health issue.

Trauma: An extremely upsetting and emotionally taxing incident or encounter that has detrimental long-term ramifications.

For important terms on Schizoid Personality Disorder that are used throughout the book, this glossary is a useful resource.

Printed in Great Britain
by Amazon

44101384R00036